THE TRACKS and LAND-
FALLS *of* BERING AND
*CHIRIKOF* ON THE NORTH-
WEST *COAST of* AMERICA.

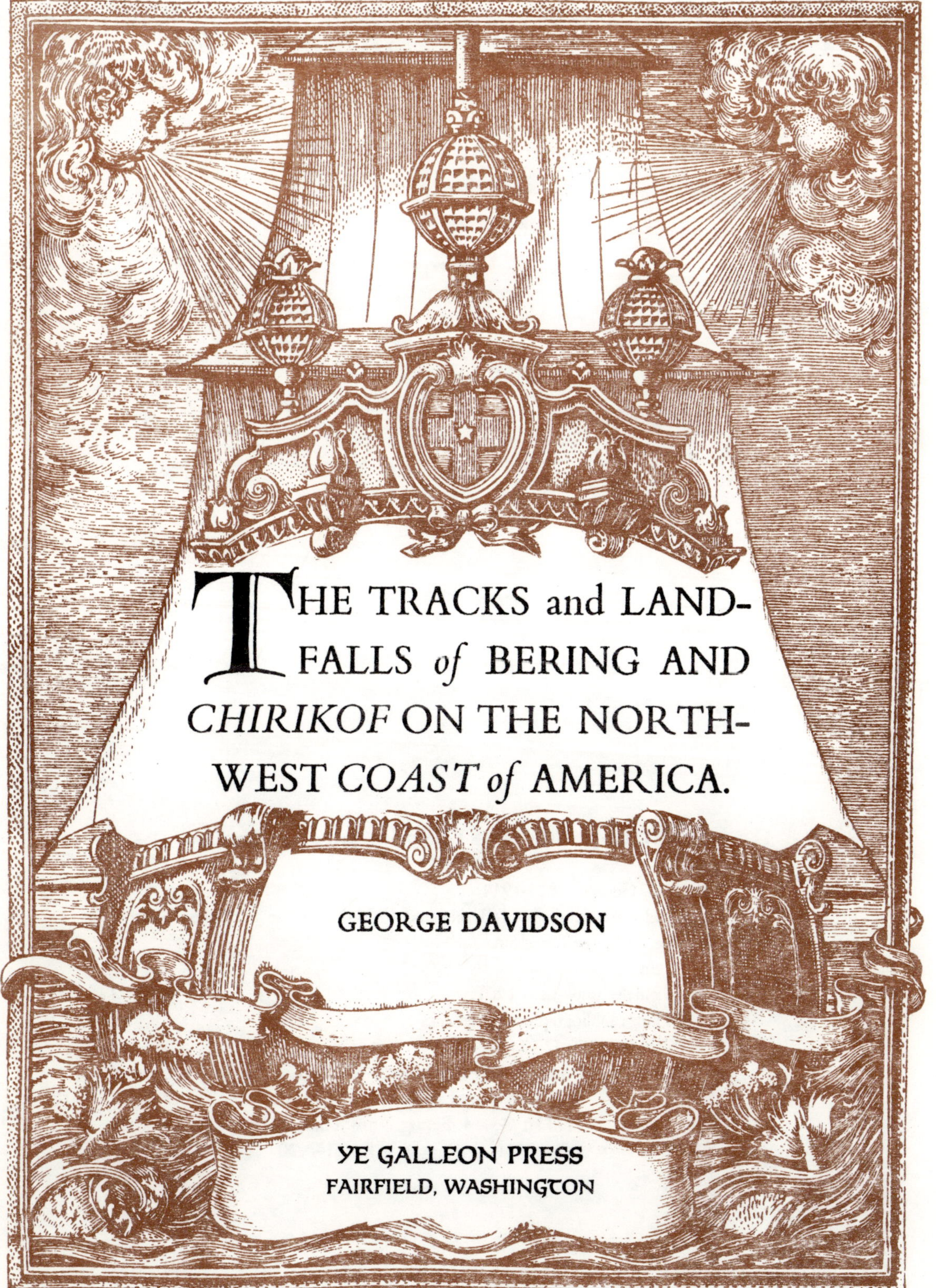


THE TRACKS and LAND-
FALLS of BERING AND
CHIRIKOF ON THE NORTH-
WEST COAST of AMERICA.

GEORGE DAVIDSON

YE GALLEON PRESS
FAIRFIELD, WASHINGTON

**Library of Congress Cataloging-in-Publication Data**

Davidson, George, 1825-1911.
    Tracks and landfalls of Bering and Chirkoff on the northwest coast of
America / George Davidson.
        p. cm.
        Originally published: 1901.
        Includes bibliographical references.
        ISBN 0-87770-527-5
        1. Alaska — Discovery and exploration — Russian.  2. Northwest Coast of
North America — Discovery and exploration — Russian.  3. Kamchatskaia
ekspeditsiia (2nd : 1733-1743)  4. Bering, Vitus Jonassen, 1681-1741. I. Title.
F907.D23              1994              979.8'01–dc20              94-2736

# PREFACE

George Davidson (1825-1911) could be introduced under any one of many titles as astronomer, scientist, geodesic coast surveyor or prolific writer. He distinguished himself in whichever discipline he entered. His intellectual curiosity, personal drive and painstaking research resulted in many books and articles of permanent value. These published works plus his coast surveys, and his associations with scientific societies made him highly respected by his associates and fellow scientists.

*The Directory for the Pacific Coast* he wrote was most useful for early mariners and pilots on the Pacific Coast in the days when marine charts were comparatively few and primitive. This work was called for many years the *Davidson Bible*. Besides giving exact locations of navigating hazards and hydrographic reports this book included the history of the earliest explorations and the naming of points, bays, coves, etc. of the Pacific coast from Alaska to California.

George Davidson was born in Nottingham, England May 9, 1825. At the age of seven he came to Philadelphia, Pennsylvania with his parents where he attended Central High School and Girard College. While still a student he was appointed as an assistant at the college astronomical observatory. He then entered a field of science in which he was engrossed for over sixty years. In 1845 he entered the United States Coast Survey. The first five years he was engaged in geodetic work, surveying, making meteorological and astronomical observations and conducting triangulations on the Atlantic seaboard. In 1850 he was assigned to San Francisco to assume the same duties he had been engaged in on the eastern coast.

When Davidson arrived in the West the navigation charts at the time of the Gold Rush were primitive or non-existant. The mariners and pilots had to rely mostly on early explorers' charts and observations. Davidson then began the mapping of the Washington, Oregon and California coastlines, and later the Alaska coast, to aid the vast shipping that was taking place at the time. Because roads did not exist in many primitive areas he and his associates had to use a sailing brig to work from to establish definite magnetic variations, landmarks, capes, bays, shipping hazards and lighthouse sites. He conducted extensive surveys of the bays of California from Trinidad and Humboldt in the north to San Diego in the south. Also he surveyed the mouth of the Columbia River and the Oregon and Washington coast to the Puget Sound.

The California Academy of Sciences was established in 1871. Davidson was a charter member and the only president up to 1887. In 1870 he was appointed a professor of geodesy and astronomy at the University of California, at Berkeley. He kept his association with the University until in old age his eyesight failed and he resigned.

Davidson's interest in astronomy was not only centered in his personal observations, but he enjoyed interesting others in that field, inviting students and friends to his Lafayette Square observatory. His most outstanding effort in this area was the influencing of James Lick, the San Francisco millionaire, to finance the Lick Observatory. On its completion in 1888 it was considered "the world's most useful instrument in that field of science."

Another very practical achievement of Davidson was his measurement of the Yolo and the Los Angeles Base-lines "upon which all distances in the extensive triangulation of the State of California depend."

He received many honors in recognition of his scientific work and writings. Both Presidents Cleveland and Harrison appointed him to important commissions. He belonged to a goodly number of scientific societies and academies. In 1910 he received the honorary degree of LL.D. from the University of California. Other scientists also honored him by designating physical features of the coast in his name. Three mountains bear his name: Mount Davidson in San Francisco; a mountain in the Virginia Range of Nevada; and one on Nagai Island of the Alaska peninsula. There are also a glacier, an inlet and a bank in Alaska, a submerged reef in the Rosaria Strait and off California the Davidson Seamount are all named in his honor.

The life and work of George Davidson spanned exciting times on the Pacific Coast from the Gold Rush era through and up to the beginning of the Twentieth Century. In all these years he led an active life in his field-work and at his desk. In the field he was physically as active as any of his subordinates, asking no one to undergo hardships or dangers he himself would not undertake. At his desk he produced some 135 published writings on scientific subjects for newspapers, magazines or scientific journals.

Edward J. Kowrach<br>
Veradale, Washington<br>
April 4, 1983

# The Tracks and Landfalls

OF

# BERING AND CHIRIKOF

ON THE

# Northwest Coast of America.

---

From the Point of Their Separation in Latitude 49° 10´,
Longitude 176° 40´ West, to Their Return
to the Same Meridian.

June, July, August, September, October,
1741.

GEORGE DAVIDSON

PRESIDENT OF THE GEOGRAPHICAL SOCIETY OF THE PACIFIC.

PRIVATE PUBLICATION

PUT IN PRINT OCTOBER 31
1901

PRESS OF
JOHN PARTRIDGE, Stationer and Printer
306 California St., S. F.

# THE TRACKS AND LANDFALLS OF BERING AND CHIRIKOF ON THE NORTHWEST COAST OF AMERICA, FROM THE POINT OF THEIR SEPARATION IN LATITUDE 49° 10′, LONGITUDE 176° 40′ WEST TO THEIR RETURN TO THE SAME MERIDIAN. JUNE, JULY, AUGUST, SEPTEMBER, OCTOBER, 1741.

GEORGE DAVIDSON.

*Read in part before the Geographical Society of the Pacific, June 29th, 1898.*

---

## CONTENTS.

CONTENTS—Continued.

INTRODUCTORY.

It is many years since we commenced the identification and reconciliation of the landfalls of the early Spanish and English navigators on the Northwest Coast of America; especially those of Ulloa, Cabrillo, Ferrelo, Drake, Vizcaíno and Aguilar, from 1539 to 1603. Following their heroic achievements was a lull of Spanish exploration on this Coast for one hundred and sixty-six years. Then came the long series of Spanish discoveries and surveys from 1769 to, and overlapping the explorations of Cook, La Pérouse and Vancouver, from 1778 to 1794, which had been prompted by Spanish activity.

In that long interval there were two important and remarkable expeditions made by the ambitious and irrepressible Russians in the North Pacific which led to Bering's discovery of the East Cape of Asia at Bering Strait in 1728; the charting of the Kurils and their relation to Japan by Spanberg in 1738-'39; and the discovery of the southwest coast of Alaska, and part of the great chain of the Aleutian Islands in 1741. Moreover the latter experience of the St. Peter and the St. Paul wiped from the Northwest Pacific, the mythical "Gamaland" of De l' Isle's map; the "Grand Isa. di Jezo e lunga" of Dudley's Arcano del Mare 1647, only three hundred nautical miles from the Coast of Oregon in latitude 46°, and the "I : di Jezo," of the earlier München MS. chart, only one hundred and eighty nautical miles from Oregon in the same latitude.

These Russian expeditions demanded far greater labor, time and endurance than those of Spain, England or France.

The literature which we have concerning the achievements of Bering and Chirikof, so far as we can reach it upon this Coast, is very meagre, and not satisfactory: so that it seemed almost impracticable to reconcile all their tracks and landfalls. Their longitudes were worthless, for they differed 13° or 400 nautical miles; the latitudes were not always reliable; the descriptions of the coasts were not consistent and wholly lacked details and elevations; while the dead reckoning was delusive, and the currents were an unknown quantity, and treacherous. We know comparatively little of the currents to this day.

Moreover, among some writers there has been quite an exhibition of feeling or adverse criticism, where in reality the largest praise and consideration was due to each and every of the heroes who had helped to successfully accomplish a great undertaking without regard to personal comfort and continuous danger. Their exploits recall the bravery, tenacity and devotion of the earlier Spanish discoverers and the supreme daring and self-reliance of those archfreebooters Drake, Cavendish and Dampier.

With admiration for the Russian discoverers, sympathy with their sufferings, and in the hope of reconciling part of the tracks and landfalls of Bering and Chirikof, aided by modern charts of Alaska, and some little knowledge of the currents and climatic conditions of the Northeast Pacific, we have so far succeeded in the investigation that we are impelled to present to the Geographical Society of the Pacific, a chart which exhibits the positions of the St. Peter and St. Paul from the night of their separation in bad weather, June 20-21, 1741, to their return to the same meridian in September and October. This period comprises their different lines of approach to the West Coast of Alaska, their landfalls, and their approach and examination of part of the Aleutian Islands.

We trust this effort may incite others with larger means and facilities to disentangle the whole of their tracks.

## The Projects of Peter the Great, and the Earlier Discoveries of Bering.

But before presenting our work in detail, it may be interesting to recall a few of the incidents of this important Russian expedition, in order to gain a fair idea of the almost superhuman labor carried on through eight years of preparation to fruition.

It will be remembered that when the Viceroy Cortés was fitting out his Pacific Coast vessels for the early exploration of the Western Coast of Mexico and California, all the essential materials of the ships, such as anchors, cables, rigging, canvass, iron work, etc., were carried across the continent from the Gulf of Mexico, (where they had been brought from Spain), to the port of Navidad on the Pacific. It was a labor that cost thousands of lives.

And so, when Peter the Great essayed voyages along the Pacific seaboard of Asia, most of the ships' outfits were carried across Siberia two thousand miles and more through the most desolate regions of the earth, and where the cold of winter is intense.

Peter the Great was an extraordinary man from every point of view, but we have to deal with him from one standpoint only. He had learned the craft and art of ship-building in England and Holland, and was therefore able to decide whence he could obtain good shipbuilders, and able seamen for service in Russia. He favored Danes, Norwegians, Dutch and Englishmen.

Vitus Bering was a Dane by birth, and he naturally took to a sea life, in which he made some long voyages as a seaman. Through the influence of one of his countrymen in the naval service of Russia, he was appointed to a place in the Baltic fleet, where he developed into a good fighter, and a bold and able commander. In the Russian service his name was Ivan Ivanovich Bering. In 1724 he was appointed chief of the first Kamchatkan expedition, the object of which was to determine whether Asia and America were connected.

It was on his death-bed in December, 1724, that the Emperor dictated the orders for Bering's undertaking. It included the building of decked boats or small vessels "at Kamchatka, or somewhere else," in which "to sail northward therefrom to the end of the Coast, which is undoubtedly America."

This expedition was unprecedented. The world knew nothing of the country or the waters to be traversed, or of their extent. We now know that the East Cape of Asia lies about 5,500 miles in a straight line from St. Petersburg. The country was inhospitable in every sense; it contained endless steppes, forests, morasses, and fields of trackless snow in winter. It embraced the pole of the lowest temperature on the earth. The inhabitants were sparse, and without resources. Over those unprecedented difficulties Bering was to transport enormous provision trains, and large quantities of material for ship building; but he was worthy the trust reposed in him by his Imperial master.

Emperor and Autocrat, Peter the Great died Jan. 28, 1725. Chirikof, the second in command, had started the day before; Bering brought up the rear Feb. 5th. One year was consumed in reaching Tobolsk on the Irtysch. Next year he built barges and boats on the Lena and made two thousand leathern sacks to carry flour to Okhotsk, nearly seven hundred miles distant. On the route the temperature reached minus 71° Fahr.; and the "pourga" or blizzard of Siberia is speedy death to those exposed to it. On the last of September, 1726, he reached Okhotsk. The mass of the party reached there late in October, to find a settlement of eleven huts with ten Russian families who lived by fishing. The expedition was housed in December, except that part under Spanberg which was caught in great snow storms with provisions exhausted, so that they ate their "straps, leathern bags and shoes." The rescue of the party demanded heroic qualities, which Bering put forth successfully.

We need not have given even these slender details, except to show the character of Bering and his officers. They were all men of extraordinary endurance and capacity. They were worthy of the Autocrat who had named the expedition, and left them to carry it out. It was successfully accomplished in 1728, by Bering sailing into the Arctic Ocean through the Bering Strait although he did not see the northwest Cape of America. This was the initiation of Bering, and Chirikof, and Spanberg for any greater undertakings.

## Some Pertinent Facts in Russian Political History, 1730 to 1741.

In justice to Bering, it seems pertinent to present a few facts of Russian political history during the short period from 1730 to 1741. They do not reveal the motives for the struggles among the nobility for the control of the Government ; but suggest the necessary conflict of opinions about the preliminary and continuous labors of Bering and his leading officers, thousands of miles away from headquarters; with no mode of quick communication. The wonder is, that in the fierce domestic and foreign issues of that period of eleven years, all of the expeditions were not incontinently abandoned. There would seem to have been a pervading and governing idea among those in power that discovery and exploration would extend the Empire and its influence. These troubles also point to the reason why so many complaints, threats and indignities were showered upon Bering.

Some years before the death of Peter the Great he had altered the order of succession to the throne in favor of the Empress Catherine. During the two and a half years of her reign and rule she consummated many wise ameliorations and undertakings. She died May 17th, 1727, having settled the crown upon Peter II, the son of the Czarovitch Alexei, who succeeded by the title of Peter II. He was then only twelve years old. For some time he was controlled by Prince Menzikoff who had risen from obscurity. This prince was banished to Siberia by the influence of the Dolgourki family, who took into their hands the management of Government affairs. In 1730 Peter II died, and was succeeded by Anna, Duchess of Courland, through the influence of the Senate and nobility, who set aside the order of succession established by Peter the Great and the Empress Catherine. Her reign was extremely prosperous, although there was a rupture between Russia and Turkey in 1735. Campaign followed campaign on the borders of Turkey, with the loss of more than one hundred thousand men and vast sums of money, until the treaty of 1739 was concluded. The death of the Empress took place in 1740; then followed the regency of Princess Anna of Mecklenburg, during which a new war commenced between Russia and Sweden. In 1741 the Princess Elizabeth, daughter of Peter the Great by Catherine was proclaimed Empress on the 6th of December, and in the afternoon of that date the troops took the oath.

## BERING PROPOSES A VOYAGE OF DISCOVERY AND EXPLORATION TO THE NORTHWEST COAST OF AMERICA.

In 1730 Bering returned to St. Petersburg from his discovery of the East Cape of Asia at Bering Strait. In 1731 his map was made in Moscow, but within two months after his return, when he submitted his report to the Admiralty, he also submitted a project for a still greater scheme of Pacific exploration.

Every effort was made to throw doubt on Bering's work by a body of discontents who built up charges against the truthfulness of his map. The Academy of Sciences would not use it. Intrigues, jealousies and machinations pervaded the atmosphere. Fortunately the Government recognized the map as authentic. Bering was promoted in regular order to the rank of Captain Commander in the Russian fleet, the next below the rank of Rear Admiral.

Peter the Great had been dead five years, but the Duchess of Courland, Anna Ivanova, a daughter of the Emperor's half-brother Ivan, had ascended the throne. She maintained her Court at Moscow. In April 17th, 1732, the Empress ordered that Bering's proposition for a more extended exploration across the Pacific should be executed; and charged the Senate to take the necessary steps for that purpose.

## The Senate, the Academy, and the Admiralty Enlarge Bering's Project.

The Senate departed from Bering's project and planned a triple expedition; and in the process of homologating an avalanche of suggestions from the members of the Academy of Sciences, and from the Admiralty, that body outlined, in extenso, the character of the physical, nautical, and geographic explorations to be undertaken by the expedition. Siberia was to be mapped; the Arctic shores were to be charted; the Coast of America was to be outlined to Mexico; the Kuril Islands and Japan were to be laid down. If America proved to be connected with the Tchutchi peninsula, one party was to attempt to find European colonies. To the really nautical and geographic explorations the Academy of Sciences had the influence to demand a scientific exploration of Siberia and Kamchatka. The personnel and outfit of this part of the expedition is painfully but supremely amusing, with its landscape artists, the many wagon loads of instruments, the riding horses, and the library which embraced the classics and light reading. Those persons selected were, of course, utterly ignorant of the conditions of the countries they were to traverse. This unwieldy part of the expedition looked to Bering for its comforts and conveniences; for boats to cross the rivers; for special assistance in flank examinations. He was expected to act as their dry nurse as well as leader. Yet he had no authority over this remarkably heterogeneous congregation of supposed scientific men. It would have required some one with superhuman power and angelic disposition to have satisfied a small fraction of them. We can easily guess at the inevitable results. They ceaselessly stormed Bering with complaints and counter charges; entered them and their judgments in their records; and threatened formal charges against him to the Senate. They never offered to assist him.

Von Baer says that no other geographic enterprise can be compared in vastness or sacrifice with the titanic undertakings that were loaded upon Bering, and actually carried out by him. H. H. Bancroft, in his "History of Alaska" (p. 42) says: "The second "Kamchatka expedition * * * was the most brilliant effort "toward scientific discovery which up to this time had been made "by any government." He further says that "Bering was strong "in body and clear of mind even when near sixty; an acknowledged "man of intelligence, honesty, and irreproachable conduct, though

"in his later years he displayed excessive carefulness and indecision
"of character, governed too much by temper and caprice, and sub-
"mitting too easily to the influence of subordinates." When we
read of the trials he endured, the opposition he met with, the
gigantic difficulties he overcame and the physical disabilities that
necessarily grew upon him by continued exposure, we need not
marvel if at sixty years of age he seemed to lack the vigor of his
earlier life. At the time of the organization of these great expeditions, Bering was not yet fifty-two years of age; and must have been
in the very prime of his manhood. Any but an extraordinary man
who cheerfully obeyed the orders of an autocrat would have thrown
up the almost superhuman task.

Bering must be judged by the times in which he lived; by the
character of those in authority; by the vagueness of his instructions;
by the fitness and unfitness and jealousies of the people who were
under him; by the great extent and desolateness of the country he
traversed destitute of roads and sparse in population; by the neces-
sity of his establishing iron foundries in the midst of Siberia; by his
building ships with which to make his explorations across unknown
seas with almost constant fogs; by the presence of that scourge of
navigator and sailor, the scurvy.

The difficulties to be overcome demanded a man of supreme self-
reliance, great physical ability and large resources. And it may be
asserted that until Bering was attacked by scurvy he was equal
to all emergencies. It seems impossible for any man at the present
day to put himself in Bering's place; and therefore flippant criticism
and prejudiced opinions must be promptly pushed aside as unworthy
of respect or consideration.

## The Expedition Starts in 1733.

As the period for the departure of the expedition approached, the
Empress Anna, in consideration of the distance, difficulties and privations to be endured and the objects to be gained, doubled every
salary. They were going to an unexplored country for an unknown
time, and nearly all the officers and the rank and file took their
wives with them. The Admiralty estimated the time at six years,
but the most of the people were going for sixteen, and the latter
were more nearly correct in their estimate.

On the 1st of February, 1733, the first detachment started; by
August the scientists brought up the rear and moved towards

Kazan. There were five hundred and seventy officers and men, and thirty or forty Academicians.

The meagre recital of the movement hence to Kamchatka is full of trouble, grumbling and complaints; the scientific men, the missionaries, the contractors, the Siberian authorities, and the subordinates bred incessant friction and discontent. On Bering necessarily fell all the odium attending the faults and misfortunes of this crude and incongruous mass of humanity. That he was not a Russian born added bitterness to the complaints sent back to St. Petersburg.

### Building Vessels on the Irtysch for the First Arctic Expedition.

In 1734 Bering built two vessels and four rafts at Tobolsk on the Irtysch (latitude 58°) for the first Arctic expedition which left there on May 13th, and five days later he left with the main command and the Academicians for Yakutsk on the Lena (latitude 62°) which he reached in October. Chirikof arrived in the spring of 1735 with the larger part of the supplies. Here Bering found no preparations as previously ordered by the government; yet in the course of six months he had two large vessels built for the second Arctic expedition; and these with four barges started down the Lena on the 30th of June, 1835, to cruise along the Arctic shore. One vessel was to chart the coast from the Lena westward to the mouth of the Yenései. The other was to cruise along the Arctic coast to the Bering Peninsula, and then, if it was a geographical possibility, to sail southward along the coast of the peninsula of Kamchatka. This project of Arctic exploration was planned and thus successfully inaugurated by Bering himself.

### Three Years of Labor on the Lena.

To these duties he added others. In the vicinity of Yakutsk he established an iron foundry and furnace, whence the various vessels were supplied with anchors and all other articles of iron.

It is unnecessary to enter upon the difficulties and the opposition which Bering met with at Yakutsk. Here he was compelled to wait and labor for three years. The Academicians were busy at Yakutsk, and their exorbitant demands for conveniences and luxuries led to strained relations with the Captain Commander. Unsatisfactory news came from the expeditions to the Arctic, and Bering personally superintended the sending of provisions to supply the magazines on that coast.

Charges were sent to the Admiralty and to the Senate by every disgruntled and dissatisfied officer and by the Siberian authorities. Much more money had been spent than had been expected, and the Admiralty found it difficult to supply the necessary funds. They threatened to fine Bering and to court-martial him, and they even withheld his supplemental salary for years. Hard drinking and a hundred accessory troubles, with constant wrangling among the officers and their wives must have nearly broken up all discipline. And to add to this process of disorganization the Admiralty authorized Bering's second in command, Lieutenant Chirikof, to investigate a series of charges against him. It surely required a man of nerve of steel, integrity of purpose and obedience to his original orders to stand up against such a band of gruff and unruly brawlers, gathered from all quarters of the world.

From the description of Bering's characteristics, drawn up by his naturalist friend Steller, it is possible that he held under control that audacity of command which would have promptly stamped out insubordination in such emergencies. He knew the character of the men he was dealing with. Steller says: "He was a true and "honest Christian; noble, kind, unassuming in conduct, and uni-"versally loved by his subordinates, high as well as low. * * He "was not naturally a man of quick resolve, but when one considers "his fidelity to duty, his cheerful spirit of perseverance and careful "deliberation, it is a question whether another possessed of more "fire and ardor, could have overcome the innumerable difficulties of "the expedition without having completely ruined those distant "regions; for even Bering far removed from all selfishness, was "scarcely able in this regard to keep his men in check."* Von Baer says: "The whole expedition was planned on such a monstrous "scale that under any other chief it would have foundered without "having accomplished any results whatever."*

### BERING MOVES FORWARD TO OKHOTSK.

In the summer of 1737 Bering moved forward to Okhotsk, where Spanberg had gone to build a new town. This settlement embraced a church, houses for officers, barracks for the men, magazines, a large dockyard and other buildings. The old stockaded post was

---

*NOTE. "Vitus Bering, the discoverer of Bering Strait by Peter Lauridsen * * * translated from the Danish by Julius E. Olson." Chicago: S. C. Griggs & Company, 1889. Vide pages 97-98.

four miles farther in the country.    The town was very badly located,
for even the drinking water had to be brought a distance of two
miles.

Solokoff, who did not write in behalf of Bering, says:  "Bering
"staid three years in Okhotsk, exerting himself to the utmost in
"equipping expeditions, enduring continual vexations from the
"Siberian government.  *  *  *  During all this time he was
"sternly and unreasonably treated by the Admiralty, which show-
"ered upon him threats and reproaches for slowness, sluggishness
"and disorder, for false reports and ill-timed accounts."  Else-
where he says:  "Bering was well-informed, eager for knowledge,
"pious, kind-hearted and honest, but too cautious and indecisive."
*  *  *  "Hence he was not particularly well qualified to lead this
"great enterprise, especially in such a dark century, and in such a
"barbaric country as East Siberia."

The pest of Bering's life was the infamous Pissarjeff, the
"branded" Governor who arrived at the same time and made his
quarters at the old stockaded post or fort at Okhotsk.  Bering says
he was foul mouthed and extremely offensive.  Spanberg asked
Bering for authority to go and arrest the old knave.

The site of Okhotsk was at the junction of the Okhotsk and
Kukhta, on a low, sandy, narrow delta subject to inundation.
The climate was particularly unhealthy, with a cold, raw fog hang-
ing over the region almost continually.  The party was weakened
by fevers; and in this swampy place Bering lost his health.

At Okhotsk, Spanberg pushed forward the building of two new
vessels, and the repairing of two others for his own expedition to
chart the Kuril Islands and Japan; and in September, 1738, he was
ready for sea.  In two summer seasons he charted the Kurils, Yezo,
and part of Hondo.  These expeditions exhausted the provisions
at Okhotsk; and Bering made demands upon the districts of Tobolsk
and Verkhoiansk for supplies.

### Two Brigs are Built and Sail for Kamchatka.

The timber for the construction of his vessels had to be brought
twenty-five miles, but in the month of June, 1740, Bering had com-
pleted the two ships for the expedition to America; they were
launched, and named the St. Peter, and the St. Paul.  They were
brig rigged; each was 80 feet long, 22 feet beam, and 9½ feet depth
of hold; they were each of 108 tons burthen, and carried 14 two
and three pounders.

These vessels, with a galley and large sloop, were ready to sail for Kamchatka in August, but delays prevented their sailing until September 8th. They were provisioned for twenty months, and destined to rendezvous in Avatcha Bay on the Pacific Coast of Kamchatka, in latitude 52° 53'. Here Chirikof arrived in the latter part of September and Bering on the 6th of October. The harbor had been selected by the mate of Chirikof, Yelagin, who had erected a few buildings. Bering approved the selection of the harbor, and built a fort, and a church consecrated to the Virgin Mary. The harbor was named after St. Peter and St. Paul, Petropaulovsk.

The vessels were frozen in all winter and in May, 1741, the ice broke up, and Bering could supply his ships with rather poor provisions for only five and a half months. It is said that Bering's powers of resistance began to wane after his eight years of incessant labor and anxiety, and the effects of the malarial climate of Okhotsk.

Lieut. Chirikof, the commander of the St. Paul, was well educated, courageous and straightforward; bright of intellect, and thoughtful. The cruel naval service had never been able to debase him. Bancroft says it is remarkable that in all the accounts of quarrels between the heads of the various departments of scientists and naval officers serving under Bering's command, the name of Chirikof is never found. He seems to have had the good will of every one and to have escaped all complaints from superiors.

After the vessels had left port the characteristics of both men naturally came to the front. As in some similar expeditions, Spanberg's for instance, the second in command may have been humanly anxious to make independent discoveries. This peculiarity may be traced in every similar expedition to the present day.

Bering and Chirikof were apparently doubtful about the success of the proposed voyage of exploration, because a council of officers was called to consider the best mode of procedure. This was in accordance with Russian naval practice and orders. It was a great misfortune that the representations of Louis de l'Isle de la Croyère had influence in the council. The brother of Louis had constructed a supposititious map of great islands stretching far east of Japan; and before the expedition left St. Petersburg, the Senate ordered Bering and Chirikof to consult with Louis, who was really no geographer. This was peculiarly unfortunate because the Navigators believed they should sail to the north of east; whereas the project of finding the mythical land of Jean de Gama would require a course southeastwardly. In 1738 Spanberg had sailed directly over the positions of some of these mythical lands, and Bering therefore knew that the de l'Isle chart was a fraud. Bering and Chirikof could not muster courage to contemn the mandate of the Senate. The action of the several officers of each vessel, under every conceivable emergency, was determined by the Council. The hands of the Commanders were therefore tied.

### The Two Vessels Leave Petropaulovsk for the American Coast.

The vessels were made ready to sail. The St. Peter, under command of Bering had seventy-seven officers and men including the naturalist Steller. On the St. Paul Lieut. Alexei Chirikof had seventy-six officers and men among whom was La Croyère. Each vessel had only two boats.

After a prayer service the ships weighed anchor on the 4th of June, 1741, and Bering generously gave the lead to Chirikof. They sailed in company with the St. Paul always in the lead over six hundred miles in a southeasterly direction as far south as latitude 46° 09' where they should long before have seen Gamaland. Had they sailed on their easterly course from Avatcha Bay they would have struck some of the Aleutian Islands, and thence followed that chain to the Continent.

### The Vessels are Separated in a Storm.

At their lowest latitude on the 12th of June Bering ordered a course to the N. NE., which they continued to keep with unfavorable winds to latitude 49° 30', with the St. Peter to windward, when the vessels separated during the night of June 20th–21st in stormy weather. They were then only one hundred and fifty miles south of Adakh Island. Chirikof held a course to the southward and then to the eastward, while Bering searched for his companion for two days nearly in the vicinity of the separation. A Council of Bering's officers then decided to give up further search; and unfortunately they also decided to make another search for Gamaland, and sailed south to latitude 45° 16', which was reached on the 24th. Thence the St. Peter's course was to the E. NE., according to the direction and force of the wind. ~~He~~ *She* was crossing the Pacific and soundings were useless.

After losing sight of the St. Peter Chirikof drifted to the south and southeastward for two days in hopes of meeting his commander. A council of his officers decided to give up the search and continue his easterly course.

Both vessels were now running nearly parallel with each other and with the Aleutian chain; but Bering had started two and a half degrees farther south than Chirikof. On the 26th of June Chirikof was in latitude 48°, and on the 30th Bering was but twenty miles south of that position; and thence to July 4th he made poor headway while Chirikof made good progress. After the 4th of July Bering held a course well to the NE. and Chirikof kept on his general E. NE. course. Their courses cross in latitude 50° and about longitude 156°, with Bering eight days behind; but thence he made better progress than the St. Paul. Chirikof was within 840 miles of his landfall, and Bering about 780 miles from his. Bancroft says that Bering found bottom at 150 to 200 fathoms, but the Pacific is here over 2,000 fathoms in depth.

## The Different Courses of the Vessels.

From the crossing of the tracks their courses lay about one hundred miles apart and nearly parallel for about five hundred miles, when Bering hauled his course sharply to the N. NE., and made good progress. From the projected tracks it appears that both vessels after the 11th of July had favorable winds, from the northwestward. The weather was evidently clear because Chirikof got observations for latitude on the 12th, 13th, 15th and 16th; and Bering on the 14th and 16th. As early as the 11th when he was yet two hundred and forty miles from land Chirikof had noticed signs of land in driftwood, seals, and gulls; a not unusual condition in that region. The land he was approaching is about 3,000 feet in height, bold and densely wooded from the water to nearly 2,500 feet above the sea. The land which Bering was approaching was the great glacial slopes in front of the St. Elias Range whose crest line is about thirty miles back from the moderately low seaboard.

## Chirikof Makes the First Landfall; His Progress Therefrom.

During the short night (7 hours 16 min.) of the 14th and 15th of July, Chirikof sighted the moderately high land of the west coast of the Archipelago Alexander, in latitude 55° 21′ by estimation. At daylight with calm, clear weather the vessel had 60 fathoms of water at an estimated distance of three or four miles from the bold wooded shore of Cape Addington, "a conspicuous promontory," behind which the hills attain an elevation of 1,500 feet, and are visible over forty miles from seaward.

The ocean current here runs to the northward, and although the weather was calm the brig drifted to latitude 55° 41' by observation at noon. This would place the vessel ten miles S. SW. from Coronation Island which rises 900 feet above the sea, and has been seen at a distance of thirty-five miles by Douglas. Chirikof was close to the land with good water under his keel and would see some of the deeper indentations of the Coast; and this probably induced him to lower a boat which failed to find a landing place, or to allure out any canoes, if there had been any native villages. He reports no exhibitions of smoke, and at that season the Indians were probably at other and inside localities fishing for salmon. All these shores are bold, high and rocky; covered from top of cliff to summit with timber, and exposed to the full swell of the Pacific. Although deep bays make into the high land, and great straits run to the northward, yet the overlapping of capes and points, the mountainous land immediately behind the outer coast, the apparently unbroken cliffs and the absence of clean, white sand beaches would make the careful Commander wary of getting in too close with his vessel.

As the St. Paul passed Coronation Island, Chirikof had a group of small rocky islets on his port bow; but he very likely passed inside of them because the broad opening of Chatham Strait was on his starboard bow, and offered the vessel plenty of sea room. This group was named the Hazy Isles by Dixon in 1787; and on Russian charts they are designated the Tumannoi or Misty Islands. The St. Paul ran northwestward parallel to the coast and doubtless shortened sail, headed off shore and laid-to during the night of the 16th, which ended with rain and fog. The vessel was under the steep, high, wooded ridge north of Cape Ommaney where the elevation is 2,400 feet, and which Vancouver afterwards saw at a distance of fifty-seven miles. That is the Cape which La Pérouse named Tschirikoff in honor of the discoverer; but this headland was hidden from the St. Paul.

On the 17th at noon Chirikof estimated the vessel to be in latitude 57° by dead reckoning. He had no observation, and according to this assumption the St. Paul had made ninety miles in twenty-four hours; and she should then have been up with the remarkable, highly colored, volcanic cone of Mt. Edgecumbe, 2,855 feet above the sea; and to the eastward and southeastward of which stretched the deep, broad, extensive Sitka Sound.* From Cape Ommaney to the southwest point of Sitka Sound the high, wooded coast line is indented by numerous bays, large and small; but the shores are very rocky, covered with timber to the water's edge, and backed by high mountainous ridges also wooded. The entrance to Port Banks or Whales Bay is in latitude 56° 34'; and there is another called Rocky Bay just north of it. Both are readily made out by a vessel well in with the land. Thence northward to Sitka Sound the coast is guarded by numerous outlying rocky islands and islets.

Sitka Sound is a great indentation of about one hundred and fifty square miles in this bold coast; the opening to the southwest is eleven miles wide; and the depth to the northeastward is about fifteen miles to the farthest wooded islets that are not distinguishable from the main land of Baránof Island, upon which the town of Sitka is situated. The depth of water is very great across the entrance to this Sound, and there is no anchorage unless very close under the rocky shores south and southwestwardly of Mount Edgecumbe.

If the St. Paul was close under the shores south of the Sound, the high, rocky, wooded cliffs of Cape Edgecumbe were ten miles to the westward and twelve to fifteen miles distant.

## A Terrible Disaster Befalls Chirikof and His People.

We have been thus explicit of the appearance of this Sound because on the 17th of July, at the entrance to what he designated a great bay in latitude 57° 15' (Bancroft p. 69) Lieut. Chirikof, being in need of fresh water, sent the mate Abram Mikhaïlovich Dementief ashore with the long boat, manned by ten of his best men. She was provisioned for some days, furnished with guns and other arms, including a small brass cannon. It would thus appear that by carrying provisions for some days, and being well manned and armed, an exploration of some distance into a large bay was contemplated. They were given circumstantial instructions, and how they should communicate with the ship by signals. The boat was seen to row behind a small projection of land, and Chirikof's report

---

*Note—"The Coast Pilot of Alaska (First part,) from the Southern Boundary to Cook's Inlet, by George Davidson, Assistant U. S. Coast Survey, 1869, Washington; Government printing office, 1869." 8-Vo. p. 251, with illustrations. Pages 116 et seq.

states that a few minutes later the preconcerted signal was observed. Chirikof concluded that the boat had gotten to shore safely; but no other signals were received that day. Several days passed without the return of the boat, but signals were observed from time to time to mean that all was well. At last Chirikof and his people thought the boat had received damage, and could not return; therefore it was determined to send the small and only remaining boat ashore with the boatswain Sidor Savelief and several men, among whom were the carpenter and a caulker, with the necessary implements and materials to assist Dementief, and to repair his boat. This was on the 21st, and the strictest orders were given that when the necessary assistance had been given to the mate, one or both boats should return immediately. The movement of this boat was anxiously watched; she was seen to land, but no preparation for a return could be observed. In the meantime a great smoke was seen rising from the point around which the long boat had disappeared.

The day and night were passed in great anxiety, but great was their relief next morning when two boats were seen to leave the shore and move toward the St. Paul. One was larger than the other and no one doubted but that Dementief and Savelief were returning. The Captain ordered all hands on deck to make ready for quick departure. During this active preparation little or no attention was paid to the approaching boats which, while yet at some distance, had discovered that there was a large number of men on the St. Paul; so they ceased paddling, stood up, and shouting with a loud voice Agaï! Agaï!* quickly retreated towards the shore. Gradually the full force of the calamity fell upon Chirikof, who bitterly condemned himself for permitting his sailors to appear on deck in such numbers as to frighten the savages, and thus prevent their seizure and an exchange of prisoners. He believed his men had all been seized and murdered, or were held for a worse fate; more likely they were held in slavery. He was on an unknown and dangerous coast, he had no other boat, and his numbers were reduced. To increase his duties and anxiety a strong west wind sprang up and forced him to weigh anchor and seek an offing. He was warmly attached to the men who had been eight years with

---

*NOTE—Through the kindness of Captain Gustave Niebaum of the Alaska Commercial Company, and Hon. Edward de Groff, Commissioner in the Department of Justice, and Agent of the Company at Sitka for many years, the latter is endeavoring to obtain from the Koloshians their traditions of this whole affair, of which we have given whatever information we could condense. Two of the most intelligent Indians have taken much interest in the matter and have promised to interview all the old and trustworthy members of their tribe when they come in from their summer work. (Sept. 1901.)

him, and was loath to leave the scene of the disaster. He cruised off and on for three or four days, and so soon as the wind permitted he again approached the point which had proved so fatal to his undertaking.

A council of sea officers decided that further attempts at geographical discovery were impracticable, and that the vessel should return to Kamchatka. With his own hand Chirikof added to the minutes of the Council, "were it not for our extraordinary misfortunes there would be ample time to prosecute the work." The St. Paul was then headed to the northwest with the high bold coast in full view.

## In What Bay Were the Boats and Men of the St. Paul Lost?

The position of this large bay where the terrible disaster overtook Chirikof is a matter of geographical interest, and may properly be investigated at this part of our examination. He had observed for latitude on the 16th in 55° 41′ and for the next ten days his charted positions depended solely upon dead reckoning. We are therefore not compelled to assume his given latitude of 57° 15′ as absolutely correct. It is doubtful whether he could determine his dead reckoning within fifteen miles a day, with his dull sailing vessel, and the probability that as a prudent commander he laid-to at night and in heavy fogs.

The currents upon this part of the Coast are not yet known from regular and systematic investigations. In normal weather at that season of the year, a vessel moderately close in shore would be set to the northward parallel with the coast. If strong northwest winds prevailed this inshore eddy current would probably be largely overcome or even reversed. The Monthly Pilot chart for the North Pacific gives the shore current towards the northward in July.

There is no "Great Bay" in latitude 57° 15′ that would require some days to examine unless it be in the somewhat obscure opening of Salisbury Sound which lies between latitudes 57° 18′, and 57° 22′. This is the "Bay of Islands" of Cook which opens at the deepest bend of a retreating shore line with high, timbered mountain sides beyond; and which does not present the broad, deep prospect to the eastward and northeastward that Sitka Sound opens to view.

La Pérouse and Vancouver passed it without remark, and so have many of the early fur traders, English and American.

In our judgment the disaster occurred in Sitka Sound. As Chirikof's vessel approached it from the southeastward the shores of this large Sound retreated many miles to the eastward and northeastward, and was backed by snow capped mountains reaching over three thousand feet elevation that brought out its extensive features.* Cape Edgecumbe stretched out more than ten miles to the westward as if to bar his progress; the notable volcanic peak of Edgecumbe rose sharply to 2855 feet; and along the outer coast beyond was the yet unknown. This therefore would appear to have been his opportunity for protection from the northwest winds and the everlasting swell of the Pacific from the same general direction. Chirikof's vessel would at once experience smoother water as she got under the lee of Cape Edgecumbe; and when a mile or two southeast of the Cape, he could not help noting the protection of White Point, or the Point of Shoals, seven miles to the eastnortheast of Cape Edgecumbe.

As the vessel worked under the lee of Cape Edgecumbe, she would find anchorage in twenty fathoms of water about half a mile east of its southernmost projection (now named Sitka Point), and one-third of a mile from the cliffs to the westward. From this position the Island of St. Lazaria four miles to the eastward would be open from the southern line of cliffs, but Chirikof could see the smoke from a fire started at the anchorage inside that point where he might reasonably expect to find natives, whereas the physical conditions along the high, rocky and exposed southern face of Edgecumbe are wholly unfavorable for Indian settlements. Upon the outer coast the native resorts were sparsely distributed. All that the Indian needed was more easily within his reach in the hundreds of miles of the great interior straits and bays of the Archipelago Alexander.

Moreover in the history of Sitka Sound it is well known that the natives of this region have been powerful, overbearing and aggressive. At one period they nearly drove the Russians from these waters; and they retained their warlike reputation to the occupancy of the country by the United States. We can therefore understand that they were prompt to resent any imprudence or fancied ill treat-

---

*Note—Examine work cited p. 19

ment by a body of strangers. It is not improbable that they had traditions of Japanese wrecks on their coast and counted upon a fresh batch of slaves and the plunder of the brig.

Of course there is a bare possibility that this disaster may have occurred more nearly the latitude of 57° 15′ than under Edgecumbe in 56° 59′. If so it should have been in the comparatively small, open bay of Guadalupe of Heceta, 1775. An examination of the authorities who have coasted in this vicinity will more strongly point to Sitka Sound as the Great Bay of Chirikof.

In Mr. Thomas Jefferys' translation of Müller's account of Russian discoveries upon the northwest coast of America (1761), he makes the statement that "the coast made by Capt. Tschirikow, was steep and rocky, without any islands, wherefore he did not dare to approach it, but anchored at some distance therefrom;" p. 40. He then gives the details of the landing of the long boat; and on the accompanying chart (1762), drawn up by Jefferys there is the legend, "Capt. Tchirikow's landing place. Lat. observed 56ᵈ 36′:" thus confounding two events; that of the 16th with that of the 17th. Jefferys gives no indication of a bay in the map referred to, nor in the one which he says is a republication of that issued by the Academy of Sciences of St. Petersburg.

On the 17th of August, 1775, Don Bruno de Heceta, in the Spanish discovery schooner Sonora, after describing Mt. San Jacinto (Edgecumbe) and Cape Deception, continued his course along the coast to the northwestward, and anchored for one day in 50 fathoms of water in the northeastern part of a bay which he named Guadalupe; and he says the shores are very steep and wooded, and the water excessively deep. He did not see any canoes or Indians, and was very glad to get from so dangerous a position✗ He places this bay in latitude 57° 11′. Surely Chirikof would not have anchored here, and fitted out a boat for exploration under such conditions.

In 1786 and '87 Captains Portlock, Dixon, Meares and others were fur trading on this northwest coast; and when under the immediate shores, were constantly seeking for bays and inlets that they might meet natives for the purposes of barter. Dixon, when ten miles to the westnorthwest of Cape Edgecumbe (September, 1786, p. 75) steered along the coast to the northwestward in hopes of finding the Bay of Islands of Cook (1778), which the latter had crudely indicated on his chart as being twenty miles north of Cape Edgecumbe. Vancouver has placed it in 57° 22′. This is the latitude

✗ When leaving he saw 2 canoes with 2 men & 2 women

of Kloacheva or Salisbury Sound, and the strait of Olgi of Tebénkof.
Dixon says that he "could not fall in with such a place to the west-
"ward of the Cape. That part of the coast which we examined
"forms a kind of shallow bay, but affords not the least shelter for
"any vessel to lay at anchor, neither could we perceive the least
"sign of inhabitants."

In June, 1787, Captain Dixon approached Cape Edgecumbe from
the northwestward, and when a mile off the Cape he "opened a
"very large and extensive bay which had every appearance of an
"excellent harbor." This he named Norfolk Sound, the Sitka
Sound of to-day. He sailed along the south shore of Edgecumbe,
outside of Lazarus Island, and around the rocky shoal off the southeast point of Kruzof island, which bears eastnortheast seven miles
from Cape Edgecumbe, and which he named Whites Point. Then
he hauled in sharply to the northward one mile and three-tenths to
a moderately secure anchorage in eight fathoms of water over a
sandy bottom, from which location a stream of water opened abreast
the vessel. It is open to the eastward. He gives a sketch of the
shore from the cape to this anchorage. Here he traded for ten days
with a lot of the sharpest thieves he had met on the coast. At one
time one hundred and seventy-five natives were counted on and
around the ship. As we have said before, a vessel lying at anchor
under Sitka point could readily see smoke from a fire started near
this location.

Three months later, that is in August, 1787, the long boat from
Captain Portlock's vessel then anchored in Portlock Harbor in latitude 57° 46', came southward through Salisbury Sound and through
the narrow and shallow channel of Soukoi or Dry Inlet, along the
east side of Kruzof island, into the northern part of Sitka Sound,
and anchored near the previous anchorage of Dixon. The experience of this party with the natives was similar to that of Dixon's.
For two days they were anchored well off the shore in twenty-eight
fathoms of water, and when about to depart the natives cut their
cable whereby the anchor was lost. For this act the rascals were
punished by the destruction of two large canoes.

In 1786 La Pérouse recognized a small bay north of Edgecumbe
on the ocean coast and retained Heceta's name thereto.

In 1794 Vancouver was coasting close along the shore north of
Cape Edgecumbe and has noted upon his chart a slight indentation
of the shore in latitude 57° 11', which he named Port Mary.

In the Russian atlas of Tebénkof, 1848, he places in that position a bay about three miles wide and nearly half as deep, but he exhibits no soundings therein. He retains Vancouver's name.

On the Admiralty chart No. 2337 of 1854, this indentation is called "Shelikova (Silk) Bay, Port Mary of Vancouver." It presents no details and no soundings. In 1867 we learned that there was a portage to this bay from the eastern shore of the Island (Kruzof) two or three miles NW. of Port Krestov, but we have no knowledge of any Indian settlement on the ocean bay. The direct distance across, through the timber with dense undergrowth is about four miles.

In the last few years the U. S. Coast and Geodetic Survey has made a topographical and hydrographical survey of this bay and places its northern point in latitude 57° 10'. The entrance is 3⅓ miles wide, north and south, and 2½ miles deep. The north and northeast shores are bounded by many rocky islets. There is no sign of an Indian village; and from any position in the approaches all the shores are in full view.

These descriptions of explorers, both as to the appearance of the Coast, and the character of the natives, seem to fortify our judgment that Sitka Sound was the place where the discoverers lost their lives. Cape Edgecumbe at the NW. point is in latitude 56° 59½'.

## The Cruising of the St. Paul after Leaving Sitka Sound.

We now return to the cruising of Lieut. Chirikof.

On the 26th of July he observed for latitude in 58° 21' not over twenty-five miles from the coast under Mt. Crillon (12,713 feet), Mt. Lituya (11,832 feet) and Mt. Fairweather (15,294 ft.). He was then within the arc of visibility of Mt. St. Elias, 18,024 feet. From that date to August 1st his positions are well governed by the latitudes observed on those dates and also on the 28th, by his plotted courses, and by his distance from the land. On the 28th in latitude 58° 48' he was only one hundred and ten miles SW. by S. from Mt. St. Elias, and seventy-five miles from the nearest shore; and he had just crossed the track of Bering between the 16th and 17th of July. The weather was cloudy and the great St. Elias range must have been hidden.

On the 29th, in cloudy weather, he was thirty-five miles south of Kayak Island, and reached his highest latitude in 59° 16', accord-

ing to our adjustment.   He was still well within the arc of visibility of Mt. St. Elias.   He made a  good run to the westsouthwestward between the 29th and 30th, passing about twenty miles southward of Middleton or Otchek island which Bering had passed on
the 21st about thirty miles to the northward.   The island is estimated to be two hundred feet high, very flat topped, and in good
weather would be on the horizon from a ship's deck at twenty miles.
On the 30th the St. Paul probably hauled up to the northwest under
the southeast shore of the Kenai Peninsula.   On the 1st of August
he was by observation in latitude 58° 45', and less than twenty
miles southeastward from the extremity of the high, rocky coast of
the Kenai Peninsula, which he had in full view.   In this governing position, with a clear sky and horizon, he could have seen the
Barren Islands (2,000 feet,) nearly west, the Four Peaks of Cape
Douglas (9,000 feet) due west, and probably the highest part of
Afognak Island thirty-five miles to the southwest.   He was off the
Isla de Regla of Arteaga and Bodega (Aug. 2, 1779); the Cape
Elizabeth of Cook and the later geographers.

The great recession of the coast to the northwest, at the entrance
to Cook's Inlet, and the northern entrance to the Shelikof Strait to
the southwestward, would have appeared to him as great gulfs
which he would prudently avoid.   In our adjustment we place the
St. Paul in latitude 58° 49 and longitude 149° 12'.   Soon after he
left it he could have seen the Volcano Iliamna, 12,066 feet high,
and one hundred miles distant to the northnorthwest.


## The Approach and Landfall of Bering—Mt. St. Elias—

### The Progress of Bering.

In the last named position we leave Chirikof for a time, and follow the course of Bering approaching the coast from his observed
position on the 4th of July, when he was in latitude 48° 05' by observation, and in longitude 160° W. by our adjustment.

About this time Bering was quite fortunate in his latitude observations: he observed in 48° 05' on the 4th of July, in 56° 12' on the
14th, in 58° 28' on the 16th, and anchored at Kayak Island in latitude 60° 00' on the 20th.   These, considered in relation to his
northerly course, are valuable data.

As we have already stated, his track of July 8th crossed Chirikof's track of June 30th-July 1st in latitude 50° 00′ and longitude 156° 00′ W.; he was soon running parallel with Chirikof's course and continued so until the 13th. Thence his course was to the N. NE. with the ocean current carrying him to the westward. At midnight of the 15th the St. Peter crossed within the arc of visibility of Mt. St. Elias, and at noon on the 16th his observation for latitude placed the brig in 58° 28′. But before noon, when in latitude 58° 14′, the lookout reported an extremely high mountain projecting above a high range of snow covered mountains. The vessel was then thirty miles inside the arc of visibility of Mt. St. Elias; and more than 4,000 feet of the mountain was visible above his horizon. In other words the visible part showed higher than our Loma Prieta (3,793 feet) on the Peninsula of San Francisco shows from the sea when a vessel is off Pt. Año Nuevo; or as high as Mt. Diablo (3,849 feet) when seen from Suisun Bay. At noon over six thousand feet of the mountain was visible; and the vessel's course was continued to the northward for a day. Bering had light head winds and his progress was slow, so that he made little more than one hundred miles in three days. From noon of the 17th he steered to the northwestward for one day, and he was within less than ninety miles from Mt. St. Elias, with the vessel gradually approaching the shore which was then distant about thirty miles.

His track of the 17th was crossed by Chirikof eleven days later. He does not mention Mt. St. Elias by name, nor is it placed on his chart, but on Jefferys' republication of the Russian map of the Academy of Sciences it is placed in latitude 60° 12′; its actual latitude is 60° 17′ 34″.4. On the 18th the course of the St. Peter was nearly west, but she made slow progress, although she must have been under the influence of the current setting to the westward. At noon of the 19th he was close to the high, south point of Kayak island with its remarkable outstanding steeple rock (Russian, Kekur) higher than the main point. This conspicuous rock has been noted or depicted by the Spaniards, and by Douglas, Cook, Vancouver and others. It is in latitude 59° 49′, and longitude 144° 53′. Bering notes no observations for latitude in this vicinity, but he puts it in latitude 59° 40′, while Waxell's map places it in 59° 12′. It lies well within the arc of visibility of Mt. St. Elias; and Waxell's map shows "terribly high mountains covered with snow," with a cloud line between the summits and base. The highest peak is placed in 61° 05′ and perhaps these represent the western-

most part of the St. Elias range, or possibly Mt. St. Elias itself. On
the sub-chart of Chitrof they are laid down to the NE. by N.
from the Kayak anchorage.  (See appendix for the name Kayak.)


## The St. Peter Anchors Under Kayak Island.


On the 20th the St. Peter had beaten to the northward with light
airs and was anchored off the northwest shoulder of the island which
is about twelve miles north of the southern point.  In the sketch
from Chitrof's journal it is laid down nearly its true length; the
south point is named " Kap. Sct. Elias"; and the island, "Sct Elias
O."  Moderate soundings are laid down from the anchorage around
the east and north side of Steele or Wingham Island, (the Chiganik
of the natives), which lies two or three miles to the northwest of
Kayak Island; and deeper soundings to the southward of that
island and farther westward.  The St. Peter was anchored in 22
fathoms of water over a soft, clay bottom.  (See appendix for
remarks upon this island.)  Bering remained at this anchorage one
day; one boat under Chitrof, master of the fleet, made a limited
exploration for a better anchorage if needed; and the other boat
went ashore for water, taking with them naturalist Steller to give
him a chance to botanize while the sailors filled the water casks:
Chirikof on the St. Paul had run short of water before the same
date.  On the island which Chitrof visited he found numerous signs
of inhabitants; unoccupied huts constructed of smooth boards
partly carved (totems?), household utensils used by the natives,
smoked salmon, a whetstone used to sharpen copper tools, a rattle,
a small poplar box, etc.  On the island which Steller visited he
came upon two fire places where the natives had been cooking and
who had apparently just retreated, because their tracks were noted.
He found broken arrows, the wooden implements to produce fire,
seaweed, cordage, etc.  His stay collecting plants was six hours.

For the few articles taken by Chitrof and Steller, beads, knives,
iron pots, linen, etc., were sent from the vessel and left in the huts
as a sign of reparation and good will.  This visit to the island was
verified by the traditions of the natives before the beginning of the
last century.

### BERING LEAVES HIS ANCHORAGE.  UNJUST CRITICISMS.

Early on the morning of the 21st, contrary to his custom, Bering came on deck and ordered the anchor weighed for the prosecution of the voyage.  This departure has given rise to violent and unseemly adverse expressions against the commander, although the original condemnation comes almost wholly from the naturalist Steller, who was not one of the ship's officers, and not admitted to the councils except on special occasions; and in no wise was he responsible for the safety of the ship.  Quite naturally he was anxious to make collections of natural history, and it would appear from his journal edited by Pallas, that more than one summons for him to return to the ship on the 20th was made by the commander. All the water casks had not been filled but the wind was coming up from seaward, and the vessel would have to seek a better anchorage.  Moreover there was nothing to be gained to geography by a prolonged stay at such a forbidding island under unfavorable conditions.  Bering was wholly and solely responsible for the safety of the ship and her people: there was no consort to fall back upon in case of disaster.  Steller clearly disobeyed orders; he strained the personal friendship of Bering nearly to the breaking point.  In the present case a few more plants, seaweed or cordage should not have weighed one iota against the judgment of the commander; and such remarks as "pusillanimous homesickness" and the "fear of a handful of natives" that were never seen, were simply mutinous.

"According to his instructions, Bering was authorized to spend two years and make two voyages in the discovery of America; and to undertake another expedition afterwards with new preparations and equipments.  And in his explanations to the crew he called especial attention to this point.  Under these circumstances it would not have been right in him to assume any more risks than absolutely necessary."*

They were within reach of land; a wild and forbidding coast overshadowed them; and other and more favorable landings might be made when necessary.  In his consideration of all the conditions that presented themselves he must surely have recalled the interference of La Croyère that in the early part of the voyage had delayed the ships and brought danger to the expedition by his demand that they search for the mythical Gamaland of his brother's map,

---

*NOTE.—Lauridsen: p. 154.

whose vague locations Spanberg and Walton's tracks had three times passed over in 1738 and 1739.

Furthermore, the provisions of the vessel were nearly half consumed; the general movement of the wind was from the westward; and Bering himself and nearly one-third of the crew were on the sick list with scurvy. Dense clouds obscured the sky as the St. Peter commenced her return voyage, and rain fell incessantly. Bancroft well says that "dismal forces were closing in round the Dane." Even Steller admits that "the good Commander was far superior "to all the other officers in divining the future."

We believe that Bering exercised the judgment of a capable, self-reliant, far-seeing and clear-headed commander, placed in a position surrounded by adverse and conflicting conditions. Bering, as well as every other explorer and commander, has the right to be judged from the standpoint of his orders, the character of the Government, the work which he has already accomplished and what he hopes to surpass, the means and methods at his disposition, his distance from support, the character of his officers and men, his source of supplies, and especially the depressing effects of disease.

He rose equal to the emergencies of the occasion, and set aside the instructions which required him to act in accordance with the Council of officers; and assumed all the responsibilities. The Council made no protest to his plans. To judge clearly and coldly of his decision we must try to put ourselves in his place, and remember the character of the vessel, of his instruments, of his outfit, of his resources, of the weather, of the direction of the winds, of the trackless ocean, and of the terrible and inevitable consequences of shipwreck in that region. There was no soul to assist them in the hour of danger. He can not be criticized by the geographical and climatic knowledge available to us to-day.

Müller in referring to all the discouraging conditions that beset the officers and men of the St. Peter, recalls the expression of one of the former as follows: "I do not know whether there can be a "more discontented and worse manner of living in the world, than "to navigate an undescribed sea. I speak from experience, and "can say with truth, that during the five months I was in this voy-"age, without seeing any land known before, I did not sleep "quietly many hours; because I was in continual danger and un-"certainty."

THE ST. PETER PURSUES HER VOYAGE TOWARD THE SOUTHWEST.

On the 21st of July the St. Peter had made but twenty-five miles to the westnorthwest from her anchorage, and must have been within ten or fifteen miles of the low shore of the delta of the Atna or Copper River, in moderately shoal water, with high broken land ahead and to the westward, if the weather permitted him to get glimpses of it.

The proposed route of the expedition had been to follow the American coast, when discovered, to the latitude of 65° or 66°, (his latitude of the western cape of Bering strait,) but the great barrier mountains of this Alaska region precluded farther progress northward. Consequently the vessel pointed to the south of west. At noon of the 21st he steered to the westsouthwestward, and on the 22d the St. Peter was perhaps ten or fifteen miles south of Cape Cleare, the southern point of Montague Island which is in latitude 59° 46'. The island is traversed by lofty mountains. In his position, and probably from the time he left the Copper River delta astern, the soundings would range from 40 to 50 or 60 fathoms. Fortunately he was to the northward of the Sea Otter and two other dangerous reefs.

During the 22nd and 23rd, the course was to the S. SW. and the chart indicates that he was in sight of land; but Müller says the weather was thick and the coast invisible. At noon on the 23rd in latitude 58° 40' by our adjustment, the St. Peter was in the position crossed by the St. Paul seven days later. He continued his course to the S. SW. and on the 24th the vessel was in latitude 57° 45' and longitude 149° 30'. Here he would be in 150 fathoms of water, and off soundings. The course was then changed to the westsouthwestward, and it passed over the northern part of the Albatross bank with soundings from 60 to 40 fathoms. On the 25th it was decided in Council that the St. Peter should run under easy sail for Petropavlovsk (Lat. 52° 53'); and whenever wind and weather permitted to head for the north and west, in order to explore the coast they had left. Their general course would have been to the westsouthwest, had no land intervened. They were then on soundings but the wind was easterly, and thick fogs prevailed and dangers lay close under their lee. At noon on the 25th our adjustment places the brig in latitude 57° 30', about fifteen miles off the high, rocky, broken shore of Kadiak Island at Cape Greville of Cook. The St. Peter had 40 fathoms of water or less, and her course was changed to southwest, which is nearly parallel with the general trend of the shore. According to Waxell's chart the soundings ranged from 35 to 60 fathoms, and Müller says the vessel found herself frequently close under the shore. The current was perhaps carrying the vessel on her course, and with an inset effect in part due to the easterly swell.

## CAPE HERMOGENES, KADIAK ISLAND.

At noon on the 26th Bering estimated the vessel to be in latitude 56° 30′, when he saw a high, projecting point of land to the northward, distant about sixteen miles. The chart places the noon position in 56° 55′, in the midst of a space indicative of soundings; and land far distant. This cape Bering named St. Hermogenes in honor of the patron saint of that day; but we have appealed to Greek Church authority in San Francisco, and learn that the 26th of July, old style, is dedicated to St. Ermolái (Hermolaus) six days after St. Elias day. The day of St. Ermogéne is August 13th, on which date Bering was off Unalaska and out of sight of land. This landfall is the south or southeast shore of the large island of Sakhlidak,* closely set into a deep recession of the high, broken, southeastern coast of Kadiak Island, which they were skirting. Tebénkof says the former island is mountainous and barren. Its southern head is in 57° 00′. The main island Kadiak rises to nearly 3,000 feet elevation at 20 miles from the coast.

The identification of this cape has not hitherto been established.

The skeleton chart drawn up from sketches and descriptions of Bering, Chirikof and Chitrof (Lauridsen's Vitus Bering, Chicago, 1889,) does not record the name St. Hermogenes, but has a projecting point in latitude 57° 36′ dated 25th when the vessel was on soundings there indicated. Waxell's chart does not give the name, nor does Steller refer to it. In latitude 57° 25′ Waxell has a projecting head without name; but the soundings lead southward therefrom. On Jefferys' republication of the chart of Russian Discoveries published by the Academy of Sciences of St. Petersburg, St. Hermogenes is placed in latitude 58° 48′, with the adjacent coast undefined. In June 1778, Captain James Cook named Marmot

---

*NOTE—This name has been spelled differently by different authorities: Lisiansky 1805, Saltkhidak; Russ. Hydr. chart No. 9, 1847, Sakhlidok; Archimandritoff 1848, Sakhlidak; Russ. Amer. Co. 1849, Sakhlidak (Tchalitak.) Archimandritoff made the survey of the Island in a bidarka with two natives, and his spelling is to be preferred. It is the Isla de Soto of the Spanish explorers.

Island St. Hermogenes Island, and placed it in latitude 58° 18′ on his chart. On the 2nd of August 1779, the Spanish fragata Princesa, Lieut. Don Ygnacio Arteaga, and the fragata Favorita Lieut. Don Juan Francisco de la Bodega y Quadra, anchored off the entrance to Chatham Bay behind the island Regla; and state that " this point and Point Regla is the same which was called San " Ermogen by Captain Bering, and which they found to be in "latitude 59° 08′, and longitude 43° 46′ " west from San Blas. This Pt. Regla is the Cape Elizabeth of Cook. In the chart of the Spanish explorations of the Sutil y Mexicana in 1792, Marmot island is named Isla San Hermogenes.

In April 1794, Vancouver passed fifteen miles to the eastward of Marmot island which he called I. St. Hermogenes, and placed it in 58° 14′ by dead reckoning, or on the authority of Cook. The name is not on Lisiansky's chart of 1805; nor on any of the Russian charts, including Tebénkof's about 1848-'52; but it is found on the British chart No. 2173, 1853, applied to Marmot Island  This location was provisionally adopted by the United States Coast Survey in 1867, but applying the name to the south point in latitude 58° 10′.

On the 24th of July, when the St. Peter was in latitude 58° 14′ she was between eighty and ninety miles east of Marmot Island, which was the nearest land. On the 25th at noon she had made seventy miles toward the westsouthwest, and possibly got a glimpse of the land, or was warned by soundings of less than forty fathoms to haul out sharply to the southwest by south.

Lauridsen says (p. 156, Olsen's translation,) that when " in lati- " tude 56° 30′ and about sixteen miles toward the north, they saw " a high and projecting point which Bering called St. Hermogenes, " in honor of the patron saint of the day." Bering had not seen the entrance of the Gulf of Kenai (Cook's Inlet,) nor the thirty miles wide northern entrance of the Shelikof Strait between Kadiak Island and the main land on account of fogs; nor had he seen the eastern coast of Kadiak Island although he was on soundings; and therefore he thought this headland of St. Hermogenes was a contin- uation of the continental shore of which he had glimpses. " It is "represented as such on Müller's and Krasilnikoff's manuscript maps "in the Archives of the Admiralty."

From this examination of authorities we believe that the south point of Sakhlidak Island in latitude 57° 00′ is the Cape St. Hermo- genes of Bering; and that the name was erroneously applied for that of St. Ermolái.

### THE ST. PETER PASSES THROUGH DOUGLAS CHANNEL INTO SHELIKOF STRAIT.

From the 26th of July to the 4th of August, the positions of the *St. Peter* in this examination are controlled (1) by her relation to Cape Hermogenes, (2) the observed latitude of July 31st, (3) the anchorage off the northwest end of Tomano island, (Ukamok,) (4) the position near the Simidi group, (5) the soundings on Waxell's chart, (6) the courses on the Bering, Chirikof, Chitrof chart in Lauridsen, (7) and some slight personal knowledge of the currents and the depths of water.

The latitude of the 21st is reported 54° 49'; on the chart it is placed in 55° 02'.

The drawbacks to navigation in this immediate locality were very great from natural causes. The southern extremity of Kadiak Island was only thirty miles distant from their position at noon on the 26th, the low-lying Trinity Islands off the southern point are separated from the smaller islands immediately under the point, by a comparatively shallow channel three miles wide and three miles long, lying roughly east and west. The tidal currents entering and leaving the southern part of the Shelikof strait abreast these islands, are strong and conflicting; and beyond all these unknown dangers, was the dense fog hiding everything. The navigators could trust only to their soundings. Both the charts referred to have no indication of the two relatively large Trinity Islands, and therefore they were not seen. The tidal currents through the Douglas channel were reported to us in 1867 by the Russian navigators as running five knots.

At night the vessel found herself in shoal water, tossed by heavy current rips, with rain and strong winds and a dense fog or mist so that she dared not anchor. Waxell's chart gives soundings so small as ten fathoms sixty miles northeastward of Tomano Island, and therefore on the north side of the Trinity Islands.

Taking all the above conditions into consideration, we are constrained to believe that the *St. Peter passed through the Douglas channel between the north side of the Trinity Islands and the south of Kadiak Island* and the small islands immediately adjacent thereto; and on the 27th at noon found herself about fifteen miles westward of Tugidak Island in about twenty to thirty fathoms of water. From this position she changed her course sharply to the west-southwestward until she got into at least one hundred fathoms.

She must have passed dangerously near to the southwest point of Tugidak Island in the night. According to Müller she got into twenty fathoms of water and less; and hauled to the southward.

On the 28th, 29th, 30th and 31st, the St. Peter was off soundings, and on the last date Bering observed and found himself in latitude 54° 49', which we have assumed as correct in our adjustment. From this last position, with the prospect of better weather, and in accordance with the plan of procedure, the St. Peter hauled to the northwestward. The north point of Tomano Island was eighty miles distant, and of course below his horizon.

Müller and Bancroft say Bering discovered Tomano or Foggy Island on the 30th of July, but the track chart in Lauridsen clearly indicates that the date is erroneous. On the night of August 1st in a thick fog and calm weather, they found themselves in only six fathoms of water, with a strong current. They managed to get into 18 fathoms and anchored until daybreak. In the morning of August 2nd they were four miles to the westnorthwest of the northeast point of Tomano Island, which they placed in 55° 32' by dead-reckoning from the observed latitude of July 31st. Here the currents are strong and conflicting. Waxell's chart places it in 55° 20', Cook placed it in 56° 10' by dead-reckoning. Cook has an island on his chart about twenty miles S. SW. from Trinity Island, which is not named nor mentioned in his narrative. He very probably got a sight of the south end of Tugidak Island. The north point of Tomano Island is in latitude 55° 54' by our charts, and the island is nine miles long, according to Tebénkof. Bering's error is easily accounted for by the strong irregular currents and thick weather. Bering named the island St. Stephen from the church calendar August 2nd,* but by the officers it was located on the charts as Tammanoi or Foggy Island. The Aleut name is Ukamok. Cook called it Foggy Island and supposed it was Bering's, but Vancouver called it Tscherikow's I., and placed it in 55° 56'. He has the mythical island of Cook half way between it and the Trinity Island.

From this island Bering steered to the northward and westward, mostly over soundings, to about latitude 56° 30' at noon of the 3rd of August. Here he had a view of the two snow-covered peaks named, on the Russian charts, Chiginagak (Aleut) in latitude 57°

---

*NOTE—The date on which the Church commemorates the removal of his relics from Jerusalem to Constantinople in 428 A. D.

10′, distant forty miles on the southeast coast of the Peninsula of Alaska.

On Waxell's charts the higher and northern peak is placed in 57° 13′ without name; there is no name on the chart in Lauridsen; they are named St. Dolmat on the Royal Academy of Science map in Jefferys' Müller, and placed in latitude 59° 20′, or about 37′ north of his Cape St. Hermogenes. The Greek Church calendar day for St. Dalmat is August 3rd, old style. Bering was here one hundred and fifty miles to the northwestward of Chirikof's position of the 9th.

### Bering Approaches the Simidi Group.

With the high continental mountains dead ahead of Bering's course on the third; and with stormy and foggy weather and the easterly wind the St. Peter's course was necessarily changed to the southsouthwestward, and in thirty-five miles she was abreast of the eastern side of the southern part of the Simidi group, where Cowiet Island reaches 1200 feet elevation. He also had a view of the northernmost island Agayak or Aghiyuk, 1500 feet high. The former is in latitude 55° 58′, and the latter in 56° 17′.

On the Bering chart the name Endoiefski is applied to the largest island of the Simidi group which he saw to the westward on the 4th of August. Lauridsen says the group was named the Jefdok-jejeski Island which has been changed to Simidi; Waxell has no name upon his chart; Tebénkof calls them the Simidi, and names the largest one Agaiak. Bancroft says "little progress was made " among the islands in August, owing to the thick mists and con- " trary winds. As the water gave out and scurvy came the ship " once more found itself among a labyrinth of islands with high " peaks looming in the distance, the largest then in view was named " Eudokia." On his small chart he applies the name to the largest island. This Eudokia is the Agaiak of Tebénkof and its height is reported 1500 feet, whence its summit is visible from a ship's deck at forty miles. Bering was probably twenty miles to the eastward of it. In the Greek Church the day of St. Eudokiia [Eudoxia] is March 1st, one day before Bering saw Foggy Island.

### The Adjustment Between the Simidi and Shumagin Groups.

From this position to that of August 29th, when the St. Peter reached the large island of Nagai of the Shumagin group, controlled also in latitude by observations on the 8th, 18th and 28th, the St. Peter was baffled by unknown and conflicting currents, by fogs and by calms, and probably sailed not more than seven hundred and fifty miles.  In order to maintain the general characteristics of the courses laid down in the Bering chart, and yet conform to the geographical positions noted above, much care is required in the adjustment.  In the modern chart the difference of latitude between Cowiet and Nagai Islands is 1° 02′ of latitude and 3° 07′ of longitude; on the Bering map these quantities are respectively 30′ and 5°; and on the Waxell map 20 and more than 4°.  Thus it is seen that they are very erroneous in direction and distance: on the modern chart the south end of Nagai bears S. 60° W., and one hundred and thirty-five miles distant from Cowiet; on Bering's chart S. 80° W. and one hundred and seventy miles, and on Waxell's S. 80° W. and two hundred miles distant.

It is very probable that no two persons will make exactly the same adjustment; and yet there can be no material or essential differences.

There can be no doubt whatever, that the two groups of islands are the Simidi and the Shumagin of modern charts.  The charts of Bering and of Waxell are themselves conclusive; Bering's boats under Chitrof and Waxell made a seven days' exploration of the latter group; buried one of the crew there, (the first of twenty-one who died) and Waxell had slight communication with a few of the natives, among whom he saw a knife of peculiar make.  The number and general relations of the two groups are satisfaotory; Bering's soundings off the groups clinch the matter.

## The Movements of Chirikof from August 1st when off Cape Elizabeth.

At this point in the investigation it is interesting to bring forward the movement of Chirikof's vessel.  On the 1st of August she was twenty miles to the southeastward of Cape Elizabeth, and thence her general course was a little to the west of south, passing close to Marmot Island in 58° 15′ on the 2nd.  This is probably the land he sighted that day.

The checks for the determination of Chirikof's positions are few. (1) Probably two more glimpses of Kadiak Island on the 3rd and 4th, (2) observations for latitude on the 10th and 18th; (3) sight-ing the Island of Unimak and the Islands of the Four Mountains on the 4th of September; (4) and of Adahk Island on the 9th.

In such a long period it is necessary to consider the conditions of the weather from the last named date backward to the 30th of August when he took favorable winds; and to give large weight to the courses and distances which he has plotted. This we have done with some allowance for the effects of currents.

### The Two Vessels Close to Each Other for Many Days.

The independent adjustment of the courses and distances of Bering and Chirikof within the dates August 8th and 30th reveal a remarkably close proximity of the two vessels for more than two weeks. The courses cross each other several times; the winds were light and baffling, and thick weather prevailed. On the 16th of August, the vessels were probably within fifteen miles of each other. On the 18th they both got observations for latitude and the St. Paul was only thirty miles to the northwestward of the St. Peter. They were working slowly to the westward with light airs, and on the 21st they must have entered an area of calm and clouds. In nine days from the 21st, Chirikof made only thirty-five miles to the northwestward; on the 21st Bering got a light air and two days after he was forty miles north of Chirikof. Here he was baffled for four days with calm weather, and then got a fair wind, so that he ran northward and made the mountain cape of Nagai, the large, middle island of the Shumagin group on the 29th. On the 30th, Chirikof, then in latitude 52° 35′ ran with a fair wind directly west. After the 1st of September, he was within the arc of visibility of Makúshin Volcano 5,691 feet elevation, on the island of Unalaska; and continued within the arc of visibility of the successive mountains of Umnak, Four Mountains, etc. to the 12th of September, when he was about thirty miles south of Adakh Island in latitude 51° 08′, and longitude 177°W. His chart indicates that he saw the land only on the 4th and 9th of September, both of which fairly well-establish his position. We follow him no farther.

We believe the foregoing exhibit of the two vessels for more than two weeks within a limited and calm area has not before been made.

We believe this calm period was an early exhibition of the "Indian Summer," well known along the northwest coast; short, hazy, smoky and restful. It comes later in the Puget Sound region, and is full of repose. The St. Martin's Summer of the Mediterranean countries.

Both crews must have felt the benefit of this calm weather, which seems to have continued with the St. Peter through the reconnaissance of the Shumagins.

### BERING'S SURVEY OF THE SHUMAGIN ISLANDS.

The time consumed by Bering in making an examination of the Shumagin group necessarily had an important bearing upon his future progress, because it threw him later into the bad weather of September; and when he left the group on the 6th, running south for ninety-five miles; and on the 8th of September made a westerly course, he was more than sixteen degrees of longitude or six hundred miles behind the St. Paul. But the examination was so well done that no doubt whatever remains of his position. Had he merely made the land and then continued his course westward, it would have been difficult to reconcile his positions and courses between that group and the Simidi.

Lauridsen says that Bering's journal places them in latitude 54° 48'; remarking that it had the usual error of about 30' to 45' too small. His chart places the first anchorage in 55° 28'; this anchorage we identify by Near Island which lies three miles to the eastnortheast of the first anchorage under the southern part of Nagai Island. On recent charts it is in latitude 54° 56'.

Bering gave the name Shumagin not to the whole group but to the island where the sailor Shumagin died as he was being taken ashore. This was on the southeastern part of the island of Nagai where he first anchored. We find no recorded observation here; but after the examination of the group, observations for latitude were obtained at the second anchorage under the eastern side of the small, but very high island of Chernobur (1500 feet.) This anchorage is in latitude 54° 47' which agrees with the statement of the journal but the chart in Lauridsen makes this latitude 55° 15'. Müller says "these islands are situated in latitude 55° 25'"; but the northern part of the largest one of the group only is in latitude 55° 23'; and the northernmost in 55° 33'.

If Bering's observation at Chernobur Island placed him in 54° 48' he was within one mile of the latest determination.

### Bering's Health Breaks Down.—Waxell in Command.

Bering was now in a very bad physical condition with the scurvy; he rallied somewhat under the treatment of Steller, who obtained antiscorbutic plants from the shore.   Waxell was put in command. He endeavored to have some communication with the natives, but both parties were distrustful of each other.

We now follow the St. Peter from September 6th to September 24th, during which period the ship made fair progress to the south and west.   They obtained observations for latitude on the 13th, 15th, 22nd, and made the high mountain on Atkha Island on the 24th.   When she left the Shumagins she ran south to latitude 53°, and then changed her course to the W. SW.   She was apparently just outside the arc of visibility of the high mountains part of the time; but her general course was parallel to the Aleutian chain; and their chart lays down a line of islands seen to the northward from the 13th to the 24th.   With clear weather on the 22nd and 23rd, the vessel steered northward until the 24th, when, by our adjustment, she was in latitude 51° 42' and longitude 170° 40' W. distant twenty miles from the island of Atkha with its high volcanic peak Korovenskaye 4,988 feet above the sea, and visible at eighty-one nautical miles.   According to Bancroft they made the land unexpectedly, and finally escaped from its dangerous shores.

The St. Peter's course had crossed that of the St. Paul's several times, and at the last date mentioned Bering was nearly seventy miles east of where Chirikof had been on the 8th.   Müller says, that on the 24th Bering saw one of the highest snow capped mountains on the coast, and as that was the church day of the Conception of St. John the Baptist, that name was given to it.   It is in latitude 52° 24', longitude 174° 20' west; but on Waxell's chart he specifically names "St. John Mt.", and places it in latitude 53° 19'.   Waxell evidently supposed it was on mainland beyond the island they had in sight.   Jeffery's republication of the chart of the Royal Academy of Sciences places Mt. St. John in latitude 53° 30'; and Bering's position is in 51° 30'.

This mountain has given rise to dispute on account of a high mountain seen by Chirikof presumably in this region.   Müller says they computed their position to be in latitude 51° 27'; afterwards to determine the location of the coast more exactly it was estimated to be in 52° 30'; but Chirikof who had been on this part of the coast placed it in 51° 12'.   Chirikof's date for this position is given as September 20th by Müller; but his plotted latitude for that date is 52° 32'; and he was directly west of his observed latitude of 52° 30' (chart) on the 18th. This latter observation must have been erroneous because there is no land so far north. The fact is the vessels were far apart, and they saw different mountains on different islands.

About the latitude of 52°, and longitude 174° to 179° west, there are five peaks that range from 4,988 feet to 6,974 feet in elevation, and they rise sharply from the water. They are visible from eighty to ninety-five nautical miles.

If Chirikof found land as far south as 51° 12' on the 12th of September (Müller p. 55) he was under the island Amatignak in longitude 179° west; it is about seven miles in extent and 1,921 feet elevation, with profound depths of water around it. He had no latitude observations for one month and no reliance whatever can be placed upon his dead reckoning. Erroneous reckoning, and irregular currents controlled his estimates of position. At the date last mentioned Chirikof was unable to move on account of scurvy, and his astronomer was reduced to the same condition.

A few words more and we carry the St. Peter to the limit of our chart. Adverse winds from the west and W. SW. forced the brig to the southeast two hundred and fifty miles by the 30th of September. The winter winds and storms battered her to the north, east, and again to the south, where we fix her position somewhat clearly as to latitude by four observations of the 7th, 8th, 11th and 16th of October.. The ocean current, the northern edge of the Japanese Kuro Siwa, moved her to the eastward. The vessel had been driven as far south as 48° 15', about longitude 170° W.; had worked to the northward to 50° and then steered westward. On the 19th of October, she was in latitude 49° 30' and in the longitude 177° 00' directly south of Adakh Island which the St. Paul had passed on the 12th of September. What Chirikof's estimated longitude really was it is difficult to say.


CONCLUSION.—CHARACTER OF THE MEN OF THE EXPEDITION.

We have thus brought to a close the task which we imposed upon ourselves. We believe we have solved, in large measure, some of the difficulties of reconciliation in the tracks and landfalls of two heroic men who were supported by officers and men of the same character.

They were men who had overcome eight years of extraordinary difficulties, with wretched means imperfect instruments, crude methods, and that terrible scourge of the sea, scurvy, as their constant bedfellow.

They pushed into a trackless region of storms, fogs, mists and rain; of strong and unknown currents; a wilderness of islands; mountainous shores; deep waters and exposed anchorages.

They were comparatively many in numbers and crowded into small vessels that to-day would not be permitted to leave our ports. There food was coarse, and their remedies in sickness crude, and in scurvy useless. When the slow death of that disease reached them, the survivors were utterly unable to man the ships; they dropped dead as they reached the fresh air of the deck. Steller has graphically described the storms and dangers they encountered, and their dreadful slow death sufferings; these were almost incredible. Müller, speaking of the condition of the vessel and crew before the abatement of the westerly storms about October 12th, says: " Many of the ship's crew had before been taken sick, but now the "scurvy began to break out more and more; seldom a day passed "without some one of them dying, and scarce so many retained " their health as were necessary to govern the ship."

A Council of officers was called to decide whether they should endeavor to reach Kamchatka, or seek a harbor on the American coast in which to winter. The decision was to try and reach Kamchatka.

These were the men who discovered and fixed the geographical position of part of the northwest coast of America through dangers, trials and privations that compel our deepest sympathy and our unqualified admiration. They gave vitality to the long dormant energy and interest of discovery and exploration on this coast. To-day the United States is the possessor of 591,000 square miles of Alaska with its coast line of 26,364 miles and its large wealth, by the rights derived from these Russian discoveries; but the government takes no note of these heroic men who gave their lives to gain it.

"There were giants in the earth in those days."

# APPENDIX.

## BERING'S FIRST ANCHORAGE UNDER KAYAK ISLAND.

On the 6th of May 1778, Captain Cook was off the Alaska coast, westward of "Mount Fair Weather," and passing a recession of the shore marked by a wooded island at the southeast part of that indentation, he decided that it was the bay and anchorage of Bering under Cape St. Elias, and on his chart he named it Bhering's Bay. In his narrative he names it Beering's Bay. It is the present Yakutat Bay of our charts, and lies over five degrees of longitude or 150 nautical miles east of the actual anchorage of Bering.

In 1786, La Pérouse, called the Port Mulgrave of Yakutat Bay the Baie de Monti, and fixed Bering's Bay at the mouth of the All-segh' River, where there is no bay and no anchorage. It is seven degrees of longitude east of Bering's anchorage.

In 1787, the fur traders Portlock and Dixon placed Bhering's or Beering's bay east of Admiralty or Yakutat Bay.

In 1792, the chart of the Sutil y Mexicana places Bering's anchorage at the All-segh' River.

In 1794, Vancouver followed Cook and places Beering's Bay at Yakutat.

It would appear that one authority who had recognized the Bering anchorage has been overlooked.

On the 11th of February 1779, the fragatas Princesa and Favorita, under the commands of Lieuts. Arteaga and Bodega respectively, left San Blas to reach the 70° of latitude on the northwest coast of America. When north of 55° they followed the coast closely, and on the 17th of July arrived at Cape San Elias, sailed around Kayak Island, found the shelter which it afforded and declared this gulf (seno) was manifestly the exact locality which had been seen by Captain Bering.

We present the title of the MS. in our possession, and the extract covering the above declaration:

"Tercera exploration hecha el año de 1779 con las fragatas del Rey, La Princesa, mandada por el Teniente de Navio Dn. Ygnacio Arteaga, y [Virgen de los Remedios, alias] la Favorita, por el de la misma clase Dn. Juan Francisco de la Bodega y Cuadra, desde el puerto de San Blas hasta los 61° de latitud :"

"Julio 17, latitude 59° 44': 37° 12' longitude [west from Cape
"San Lucas.]   El 17 á la 1½ de la tarde se hallaban á distancia de
"una legua de la boca que forman el Cabo de San Elias y la punta
"del NE. de la Ysla inmediate, cuya canal apenas será de 3 leguas
"y á la punta del oeste de él hay dos pequeñas Yslas.

"Desde la punta del cabo vuelve la tierra por poca distancia al NE.
"haciendo ensenadas que prometen abrigos, y sigue despues al
"norueste, y oesnorueste y oeste formando un seno que manifestaba
"exactamente haber sido visto por el Capitan Berin. El mismo dia
"corrieron la parte oriental de la Ysla, y deblaron su cabeza del
"sur, donde vieron un Yslote, y peñas anegadas inmediatas á ellas.

"El Cabo de San Elias lo situaron sobre 59° 53', de latitud y lo
"consideran al oeste de San Lucas 57° 14', [this should be 37° 14',
"G. D.;] 18th latitud 59° 48', longitude 38° 21' * * *."

Tebénkof, in the hydrographic notes to his great Atlas, describes
the characteristics of Controllers Bay, the mouths of the Copper
River, etc., refers to Bering anchoring near Kayak Island, and then
makes an explanation of the name.

He says that every year the Tchugatz, (Prince William Sound,)
and the Yakootat Indians meet at the Copper River to barter; and
that the Russians first learned of the shoal water between the mainland and Kayak Island, and off the delta of the Copper River from
them.   He further states that all places east to Yakootat bay have
each four names; given by the Tchugatz, the Oogalentz, the Copper
River Indians, and the Koloshes; and that the name Kayak is
Koloshian.

---

# Biographical Note

*George Davidson, author of this historical monograph, was born May 9, 1825 in Nottingham, England, the son of Thomas Davidson and the former Janet Drummond, the daughter of John Drummond of the nearby village of Montrose, England. Thomas Davidson was the son of a prosperous textile manufacturer and owner of a mill that wove sailcloth. In 1832 Thomas Davidson decided to try his fortune in the New World, bringing his considerable family, four boys and five girls, to Philadelphia where he set up a small factory for the production of machine made lace. This venture had considerable promise but the project was later abandoned, possibly because Thomas Davidson lacked business acumen. He certainly was mechanically gifted. George Davidson was married to Ellinor Fauntleroy in Whiteport, Virginia, October 5, 1858. Ellinor seemed frail compared with her very robust, hard working husband. Their honeymoon was spent on a voyage to California, crossing the Isthmus of Panama. In the spring of 1859 Ellinor and her new husband spent some weeks living in a tent near Mount Tamalpais in California. The marriage produced two sons, George F. Davidson and Thomas D. Davidson, and a daughter, Ellinor. After a long career as a scientist, death came to George Davidson at his home in San Francisco in his 87th year, on December 2, 1911. His wife had died four years earlier and their son, George F. Davidson, eleven years earlier. Thomas and Ellinor, the other children, never married. Persons who might be interested in the life of George Davidson are referred to a book,* George Davidson, Pioneer West Coast Scientist, *by Oscar Lewis, University of California Press, 1954.*

# · published writings of
# george davidson

In the *Biennial Report* of the President of the University of California for the years 1896–1898 appeared a "List of the Published Writings of George Davidson," which contained some 135 items ranging from brief papers in newspapers, magazines, and scientific publications to bulky volumes hundreds of pages in length. These were arranged under six different headings: Geodesy, Astronomical, Instruments, Miscellaneous, Engineering, and Geography and Navigation. Four years later a *List and Catalogue of the Publications Issued by the U. S. Coast and Geodetic Survey: 1816–1902* was issued by the Government Printing Office; this lists numerous reports and other official communications written by Davidson and printed by the Survey during the half century he was connected with that bureau.

These, however, are a far from complete catalog of the products of his prolific pen in the course of his long career, for he continued to write industriously during the final years of his life, and numerous papers produced before 1898 were omitted from the list published that year.

The bibliography that follows, although it makes no claim to completeness, aims to include his more important writings in the fields in which he was primarily interested and in which he was a recognized authority: geodesy, astronomy, geography, and the history of early exploration on the Northwest Coast. Included, too—primarily to show the breadth of his scientific interests—are a number of papers contributed not only to the journals of the learned societies but to newspapers and magazines of general circulation.

Extracts from the Report of Assistant George Davidson . . . in Relation
to the Work Executed . . . during the Past Year on the Coast of California and Oregon. *Report of the Superintendent of the Coast Survey,
Showing Progress of the Survey during the Year 1852* (App. 17), pp.
101–103.

Observations Made on the Solar Eclipse at Humboldt Bay, California . . .
*Report of the Superintendent of the Coast Survey . . . 1854* (App. 40,
sec. 6), p. 127.

Extracts from a Descriptive Report . . . upon Localities on the Western
Coast of the United States from the North Entrance of Rosario Strait,
W.T., to the Southern Boundary of California. *Report of the Superin-
tendent of the Coast Survey . . . 1855* (App. 26), pp. 176–185.

Directory for the Pacific Coast of the United States. *Report of the Superintendent of the Coast Survey . . . 1858* (App. 44), pp. 297–458.
(Also issued separately.)

Directory for the Pacific Coast of the United States . . . [Revised edi-
tion.] *Report of the Superintendent of the Coast Survey . . . 1862*
(App. 39), pp. 268–430. (Also issued separately.)

Report . . . Relative to the Resources and the Coast Features of Alaska
Territory. *Report of the Superintendent of the Coast Survey . . . 1867*
(App. 18), pp. 187–329.

Condensed Account of M. Hellert's Explorations on the Isthmus of Panama, Including His Special Explorations on the Isthmus of Darien;
with Suggestions for Conducting a Future Survey. *Report of the
Superintendent of the U. S. Coast Survey . . . 1868* (App. 15), pp.
260–277.

Report upon the Geographical Reconnaissance of the Coast of Alaska;
the Physical Features and Prospective Resources of the Territory,
and Proposed Aids to Navigation. 40th Cong., 2d sess. (1868), H.
Ex. Doc. 177, pp. 219–360.

Scientific Expedition to Alaska. *Lippincott's Magazine,* II (November,
1868), 467–485.

Pacific Coast. Coast Pilot of Alaska (First Part), from Southern Boundary to Cook's Inlet. Washington: U. S. Coast Survey, 1869. 251 pp.,
8 illus.

Pacific Coast. Coast Pilot of California, Oregon, and Washington Territory. Washington: U. S. Coast Survey, 1869. 262 pp., 33 illus.

Changes of Elevation and Azimuth Caused by the Action of the Sun, at
Station Dominguez, California. *Report of the Superintendent of the
U. S. Coast Survey . . . 1870* (App. 17), pp. 178–179.

Comparison of the Methods of Determining Heights by Means of Leveling, Verticle Angles and Barometric Measures from Observations at Bodega Head and Ross Mountain, Cal. *Report of the Superintendent of the U. S. Coast Survey . . . 1871* (App. 11), pp. 154–170.

Astronomical Observations on the Sierra Nevada. *Report of the Superintendent of the U. S. Coast Survey . . . 1872* (App. 9), pp. 173–176.

The Relative Value of Great and Small Altitudes for Astronomical Observations. *Proceedings of the California Academy of Sciences*, IV (Aug. 19, 1872), 251–252.

The Abrasions of the Continental Shores of N.W. America, and the Supposed Ancient Sea Levels. *Ibid.*, V (May 5, 1873), 90–97.

Field Catalogue of 983 Transit Stars; Mean Places for 1870.0. Washington: U. S. Coast and Geodetic Survey, 1874. 33 pp.

Mesh-Knot of the Tchin-cha-au Indians, Port Simpson, British Columbia. *Proceedings of the California Academy of Sciences*, V (1874), 400–401.

Report of the Board of Commissioners on the Irrigation of the San Joaquin, Tulare, and Sacramento Valleys of the State of California. 43d Cong., 1st sess. (1874), H. Ex. Doc. 290.

Note on the Probable Cause of the Low Temperature of the Depths of the Ocean. *Proceedings of the California Academy of Sciences*, VI (Feb. 15, 1875), 29–30.

Observations on Certain Harbor and River Improvements Collected on a Voyage from Hong-Kong, via Suez, to New York. *Report of the Superintendent of the U. S. Coast Survey . . . 1875* (App. 18), pp. 293–314. (Issued separately in 1877.)

Report on the Transit of Venus Expedition to Japan. *Ibid.* (App. 13), pp. 222–230.

Report upon the Methods Employed in Irrigating Land in India, Egypt, Italy, and Other Countries. 44th Cong., 1st sess. (1875), S. Ex. Doc. 94. 74 pp., 23 maps.

[A series of eight papers on irrigation and reclamation in Japan, China, India, Egypt, etc.; the improvement of harbors and rivers; and the breakwaters of Egypt, Italy, France, Prussia, and England.] San Francisco *Evening Bulletin*, April 7, 1876, to February 14, 1877.

Geodetic Instruments of Precision at the Paris Exposition and in European Workshops. Washington: National Academy of Sciences, 1878.

Description of the Davidson Meridian Instrument. *Report of the Superintendent of the U. S. Coast and Geodetic Survey . . . 1879* (App. 7), pp. 103–109.

The Pacific Coast and Geodetic Surveys. *California Magazine*, I (January, 1880), 60–65.

Report of the Measurement of the Yolo Base [Line], Yolo County, Cal. *Report of the Superintendent of the U. S. Coast and Geodetic Survey ... Year Ending with June, 1882* (App. 8), pp. 139–149.

Examination of the Carson Footprints. *Mining and Scientific Press*, XLVII (September 8 and 15, 1883), 150, 156.

The First Ascent of the Volcano Makushin. *Appalachia*, IV (1884), 1–11.

Collection of Some Magnetic Variations off the Coast of California and Mexico, Observed by Spanish Navigators in the Last Quarter of the Eighteenth Century. *Report of the Superintendent of the U. S. Coast and Geodetic Survey ... Year Ending with June, 1885* (App. 7), pp. 275–284.

An Examination of Some of the Early Voyages of Discovery and Exploration on the Northwest Coast of America, from 1539 to 1603. *Report of the Superintendent of the U. S. Coast and Geodetic Survey ... Year Ending with June, 1886* (App. 7), pp. 155–253. (Also issued separately.)

Submarine Valleys on the Pacific Coast of the United States. *Bulletin of the California Academy of Sciences*, II (November, 1886), 265–268.

Early Spanish Voyages of Discovery on the Coast of California. *Ibid.*, II (January, 1887), 325–335.

The Magnetic Variation at San Francisco. *Mining and Scientific Press*, January 28, 1888, pp. 52–53.

Pacific Coast. Coast Pilot of California, Oregon, and Washington. 4th ed. Washington: U. S. Coast and Geodetic Survey, 1889. 721 pp., 464 illus., 1 chart.

Report on the Measurement of the Los Angeles Base Line, Los Angeles and Orange Counties, California. *Report of the Superintendent of the U. S. Coast and Geodetic Survey ... Year Ending with June, 1889* (App. 10), pp. 217–231.

Address [at International Geodetic Association, Ninth Conference, Paris, October 3–12, 1889]. *Report of the Superintendent of the U. S. Coast and Geodetic Survey ... Year Ending with June, 1890* (App. 17), pp. 721–733.

Identification of Sir Francis Drake's Anchorage on the Coast of California in the Year 1579. San Francisco: California Historical Society, 1890. 58 pp., 15 charts.

In the Matter of the Spoliation of Yosemite Valley: Report to the Honorable Secretary of the Interior. *Annual Report of the Yosemite Commissioners,* 1890.

The Discovery of Humboldt Bay, California. *Transactions and Proceedings of the Geographical Society of the Pacific,* Vol. II, No. 1 (July, 1891). 16 pp., 5 maps. (Also issued separately.)

The Discovery of San Diego Bay. *Ibid.,* III (1892), 37–47.

The Eruption of the Volcano Weniaminof, Peninsula of Alaska. *Ibid.,* pp. 59–62.

Measurement of the Irregularity in One Turn of the Micrometer Screw, and the Relative Value of Each Turn. *Report of the Superintendent of the U. S. Coast and Geodetic Survey ... Year Ending June 30, 1892,* Part II (App. 9), pp. 505–514.

The Occupation of Mount Conness. *Overland Monthly,* 2d ser., XIX (February, 1892), 115–129.

Early Voyages on the Northwestern Coast of America. *National Geographic Magazine,* V (1893), 235–256.

Geodesy: On the Variation of Latitude at San Francisco, Cal., from [6,768] Observations Made in Concert with the International Geodetic Association, in 1891 and 1892. *Report of the Superintendent of the U. S. Coast and Geodetic Survey ... Year Ending June, 1893,* Part II (App. 11), pp. 441–508.

An Examination into the Genuineness of the "Jeannette" Relics; Some Evidences of Currents in the Polar Drift. San Francisco: Geographical Society of the Pacific, 1896. 16 pp.

Report to the San Francisco Committee of Commerce on the Dangers and Aids to Navigation in San Francisco Bay and the Approaches; with a Record of 349 Wrecks and Casualties. January 9, 1896. 16 pp.

Alaska. *Overland Monthly,* XXX (November, 1897), 429–439.

The Submerged Valleys of the Coast of California, U. S. A., and of Lower California, Mexico. *Proceedings of the California Academy of Sciences,* 3d ser., Geology, I (June 26, 1897), 73–104.

A Few Incidents in My Conferences with Mr. James Lick in the Matter of the Great Telescope. *University of California Magazine,* V (April, 1899), 131–137.

The Tracks and Landfalls of Bering and Chirikof on the Northwest Coast of America, from the Point of Their Separation in Latitude 49°10′, Longitude 176°40′ West, to Their Return to the Same Meridian, June, July, August, September, October, 1741. *Transactions and Proceedings of the Geographical Society of the Pacific,* 2d ser., I (1901), 1–44. (Also issued separately.)

The Alaska Boundary. San Francisco: Alaska Packers Association, 1903. 235 pp., 2 maps.

The Glaciers of Alaska That Are Shown on Russian Charts or Mentioned in Older Narratives. *Transactions and Proceedings of the Geographical Society of the Pacific*, 2d ser., III (1904), 1–98. (Also issued separately.)

Points of Interest Involved in the San Francisco Earthquake. *Proceedings of the American Philosophical Society*, XLV (1906), 178–182.

The Discovery of San Francisco Bay; the Rediscovery of the Port of Monterey; the Establishment of the Presidio, and the Founding of the Mission of San Francisco. *Transactions and Proceedings of the Geographical Society of the Pacific*, 2d ser., IV (1907), 1–153. (Also issued separately.)

The Name "Mt. Rainier." *Sierra Club Bulletin*, VII (January, 1907), 87–99.

Francis Drake on the Northwest Coast of America in the Year 1579. The Golden Hinde Did Not Anchor in the Bay of San Francisco. *Transactions and Proceedings of the Geographical Society of the Pacific*, 2d ser., V (1908), 1–114. (Also issued separately.)

The Origin and Meaning of the Name California; Calafia the Queen of the Island of California. *Ibid.*, Vol. VI, Part 1 (1910), pp. 1–50.

The George Davidson, THE TRACKS AND LANDFALLS OF BERING AND CHIRKOF ON THE NORTHWEST COAST OF AMERICA, *was printed in the workshop of Glen Adams which is located in the quiet country village of Fairfield, southern Spokane County in Washington state. Fairfield is 30 miles southeast of down town Spokane or 22 miles south of Opportunity on state highway 27 that runs between Opportunity and Tekoa. The print is an enlarged facsimile of the 1901 version, with limited biographical and reference material added. Title page and colophon design were done by Susan Paulson, who also did the photography darkroom work, stripped the film and made the plates. Hard case binding was by Al Chidister of Oakesdale, Washington. Paper binding was by Glen Adams and Garry Adams. This was a fun project. We had no special difficulty with the work. This is the 527th book to come from Ye Galleon Press.*